The Black Art of Vampirism

Tempel ov the Black Vampire

Martinet Press

ISBN-10:0-9978363-7-7
ISBN-13:978-0-9978363-7-0

Cover design by Tempel ov the Black Vampire

DISCLAIMER
All material contained is provided for educational purposes. The author and publisher assume no responsibility for the reader

Dedicated to the Supreme Lord of Darkness and
the Goddess of Cosmic Annihilation

Salutations to our brothers and sisters of the Blood Pool
and the Black Vampire Family worldwide

Corruption Prayer

Let us rejoice in the corruption of the earth
For therein lies the fruits of our seed
The negative pulse of worthless night
Corrupting the seed and sons of light
He who stands before all thrones yet bows to none
He who comes as the enemy to burn the sons of Israel
He whose dominion entombs the cold earth
He who from the North sets fire to the world
And for corruption himself hath been given the name
Belial
For He is the Lord of Lawless Destruction
And the origin of the seed of corruption...

Ave Dominus Belial in Excelsis!

Anantadeva (Tamasi)
Lord of Primordial Darkness personified
Also known as Krsna (Black One)

Kali Ma (Black One)
Dark Goddess of Destruction
Primordial womb and annihilating energy personified

Table of Contents

The Black Art of Vampirism

The Black Art of Crime

Black Vampire Creed

I am a Vampire

A host for the Vampiric Undead.

Enemy

I renounce the ego and instead embrace my inner darkness.

Within me is present the sacred ancient bloodline, ancestral to the outer Chaos which is the all-consuming force of Vampiric Darkness.

I worship the black void of death, and exalt its precedence over life-affirming elements which are saved for the slaves of the human herd and their creator.

Vampirism is hideous, unclean and completely amoral, ever LAWLESS by its very foundation.

As an embodiment of the Black Vampire, I seek to Dominate and feed with extreme prejudice.

The Vampire recognizes His superiority over the human race of cattle, and therefore shall kneel before none.

The Blood of creation is the life, Devour it.

Vampirism is the hunger for Blood, the force of life.

Vampirism is elitist and clandestine.

All life is ripe and ready for harvest! FEED DEEPLY.

122yf
Tempel ov the Black Vampire

Nine Vampiric Aphorisms

1. The Vampire is the All-Consuming, All-Controlling; taking heed to neither the requests nor complaints of the lower slave species. The mundane human race.
2. The Vampire is Elitist and sees himself superior to all forms of life.
3. The Vampire reserves the right by the very blood running through his veins to DOMINATE all living beings, bodies of light and consciousness.
4. The Vampire makes neither excuse nor apologies for his actions, for his are the Will of the Abyss.
5. The Vampire is not part of the dayside world. He is outside of mundane moral and law. He condemns the light for he is the Shadow of the Sun.
6. The Vampire is a force of Corruption in the world, intent on dismantling and disrupting all established order.
7. The Vampire is not a life –lover, He is a life-eater.
8. The Vampire is fanatical in his conquests and makes no compromise.
9. The Vampire is inherently and absolutely a Son of Darkness.

Traditional Black Vampirism

Undertaking the bleak and unholy commitment of becoming a member of the blood family of the TOBV is an embarkation upon a very particular pathway which leads to a well-defined end goal, that being the creation of an undead entity that is a quintessential predator to the herd, humanity.

This association is a seal that will irrevocably and with a grim permanence, transfigure the individual in line with the mood and propensities of the bloodline of the TOBV, the temporal roots of which stretch back for several decades in hierarchy and the spiritual underpinnings which are cemented in the most horrific currents of which few dare to tread.

"Black Vampire" denotes an amoral vampire, an entity that is far from the purview of adherence to human law in the legal sense of the designation and equally as far from the purview of adherence to human morality in the societal sense. The race known as the Sons of Belial in the Old Testament was the wicked and lawless children of the Spirit of Darkness.

"Black Vampire" in terminology sets to distinguish this important factor from those pretenders who preface their so-called vampirism with disclaimers about what they do not do and what they do not condone. A Black Vampire is the ZENITH of immorality and is in actuality the immortal embodiment of that which is inimical to the human herd - not simply predatory but an abomination.

Such a change in constitution is not limited by the weak, limp-wristed admonitions of the variety of pseudo-vampiric, pseudo-satanic, pseudo-sinister pretenders that always have their "limits." These types of organizations are in fact the social crutches and pale echoes of personages who have been the object of our very real terror since time immemorial.

Restrictions such as "what is honourable", "what is not honourable", etc. are the vomit of the weak moralists who attempt to hold themselves up under the sign of the inverted pentagram and "obscure interests" to stop the tide of those of the human herd, stronger than they, who would trample upon them.

A Black Vampire is completely void. Void of the force of life which seeks to create, this force which is equated directly with the bloodline of the creator. Like a black hole, the Black Vampire is an embodiment of pure hungry darkness – a master of the universe, thirsting, conspiring and plotting for its great demise.

A common misconception on the true intent behind the hideous predators of night is that Vampires feed on blood not because they need it to survive, but because blood is the stuff of life. True Vampirism is not only predatory by nature, but is exceedingly evil by its very foundation.

Black Vampires are the enemies of the children of god, seeking to consume their livelihood...their blood. Vampirism is destructive, cold and indifferent to all forms of life.

As genuine death-dealers, both in spirit and in flesh, with concentrations of apocalyptic energy that serve a broad and administrative anti-cosmic purpose, we seek to trample upon all until we can revel, mouths filled with blood and stark insanity in our eyes before the coming harvest of utter annihilation, beneath the atomic mushrooms clouds, amongst the rivers of blood and carnage, at the world's end and in doing so having the satisfaction that the execution of such has been veritably our constitutional position as Black Vampires.

THE BLACK ART OF VAMPIRISM
Practical Feeding for the Initiate

It is a common misconception within the "occult" circles today that vampirism is a system of ego worship and romanticism. Furthermore, vampirism has been reduced to a bourgeois class of club goers who liberally ask for and receive blood while dressed up in 2 hours of costume and make up like a circus performer who uses a lancet to softly release the crimson nectar. It should be made clear that real Vampirism has no place for liberalism or the prudent bourgeois, nor is there any need to ask someone if he/she can be used to access blood flow (physical or astral). A Vampire assumes authority over the cattle of the world. He is a link in the chain of terror which is the global slaughterhouse, leading men, women and children alike unto their demise. Treading the earth in human form, hungering for domination, fear and blood essence.

The Vampire "harvests the fields" in numerous ways with which we will go into detail.

13

Firstly, visual contact is a lesser form of vampirism which will push your authority over your victim while you feed on them and strike fear into them simultaneously.

Feeding through eye contact is executed by locking visual contact with the victim's eyes. They will want to look away, so you must "persuade" them to continue eye contact. It is instinctual to look back at someone who has been caught staring at them; this is where the line of contact is made. Ever notice that when staring into someone's eyes it is seemingly difficult or next to impossible to look away? This is because the line of transference is locked on, like a hook in a fish. The Vampire stares deeply into their victim, looking through their eyes and right into their very soul. Once he has locked on, he penetrates the victim with the outer astral body, willing it to extend as tendrils to reach out and into their body. Begin then the backwards flow of blood current back into the central astral vortex. Envision a returning flow, willing its movement and directing it through the breath. Slowly and deeply drink in and break contact.

Next we come to feeding through empathetic touch (aka. Physical Infliction). This method has multiple layers with each layer being taken to a more intense degree.

We know the physical body is surrounded by several other non-visible bodies, one of which being the astral body. In the previous form of vampiric practice explained above and the present as being explained here, the astral body is the main tool for these applications. Through correct training of the astral body, it may be manipulated to operate separately from the physical body as well.

Beginning however on a more recognized form of empathetic touch feeding, we first look at the size of the astral body which is slightly larger than the physical body. If you are in close enough proximity to the prey (close enough to strangle), you can actually feed on them without necessarily making physical contact. The application of feeding in this manner is executed in the same way as feeding via visual contact. Lock onto the victim physically or in close enough proximity that the astral bodies may come into contact, or close enough that you may extend feeding tendrils to spike into their astral body. Begin the backwards flow of blood current rushing into you through the astral extension.

Tyrant Nirrta
122yf
Tempel ov the Black Vampire

THE BLACK ART OF VAMPIRISM
Advanced Wamphyric Application

In the previous section, we briefed on some elementary forms of blood feeding and how to effectively put them into practice. In this section we will expand on the techniques discussed in the prior section as well as go into other and more advanced techniques, such as oneiric/astral hunting, developing tendrils, emotional and psychological feeding, and the black hole effect... walking black hole.

Going back to feeding through the eyes, we will attempt to expand on this procedure. One need not make actual eye contact with victim to feed from them through their eyes; the vampire simply extends out his astral extension/tendril to his victim and feeds through it. One who becomes more skilled in this procedure may even astrally feed from several victims at once through the use of several tendrils simultaneously. We will provide a practice later on in this MS which will give the aspiring vampire a solid base for developing tendrils.

If you are to feed through full visual eye contact however, you may wish to take that to the next level via the practice of exporting negative and noxious energies straight into the victim in lieu of draining; a nefarious injection of negative vibrations which may cause sickness, panic, nightmares or mental illness. To do this, make eye contact with victim and in substitute of envisioning the victim's blood current flowing into you, focus intently on injecting a negative flow of disrupting vibrations into your victim's mind and/or vital core.

Concentrate on propelling this black venom until you can psychically feel your astral hook reach out and spike into not just their astral body, but also their psyche. Feel your hungry talons reach quite literally into their very mind itself.

If done correctly, your prey will end up very sick or perhaps worse, depending on your ability. For an example, a Blood Family member was having a "harmless" game of staring contest with an individual; little did the receiver know he was a target for vampiric feeding. The Family member waited a couple minutes before beginning his feeding. Once feeding began the vampiric personage simultaneously focused intently on sending very negative energies into the victim through the eyes, and going further, consciously projected himself right into the victim's mind implanting noxious energies. The victim, after some minutes, became awestruck and filled with fear resulting in his breaking contact. The vampire would later find that when the victim had returned home the following day, he was in a traumatic state similar to shellshock and then fell very sick and remained bedbound for the following week.

In this example we can see how "reverse vampirism" or the exportation of negative energies can be very effective in causing illness and psychological trauma.

The Vampiric Tendril

The practice of developing tendrils does not officiate overnight, one must first become not only aware of the astral body but come to know for certain of its existence via firsthand experience with it, becoming intimately aware of the outer astral dimension separate from the physical   body.

Once one has gained the ability to see with their astral eyes, has become able to visually see the astral outline of their body with regular waking eyes, has practiced with results gained the initiatory applications of feeding via sight and touch, only then should the aspiring vampire begin learning to develop their astral tendrils.

Everything that you experience, touch, taste, smell, see and hear is inherently connected, including everything that you are not capable of experiencing. The entirety of the universe and everything within it is ultimately made up of a varied spectrum of vibrational waves in a vast sea of energy. When you direct your eyes to something, the reason that you are able to see it is because light is reflecting off it and projecting that very object into the back of your eyes; therefore, everything that you see, you are at that time actually in direct contact with.

Essentially there is no such thing as "solid" matter. For instance, when you touch water you are able to reach directly through it but if you were to touch a table you would not be able to do the same. Then how is it that the table appears to be a solid object? The only reason that you are not able to reach through the table yet able to reach through water is because the frequency of the vibration of the table is higher than that of the water, making the illusion that the table is in fact solid. However, if the speed of the vibration of the table were to slow down for example, you would in fact be able to reach right through it. Everything is liquid energy in motion, vibrating to a different frequency measured in hertz.

Some may think that the above statements sound far-fetched or perhaps too grand to comprehend; they are indeed a matter of scientific fact. For those who find this information questionable, feel free to research for yourself through any legitimate scientific avenues concerning quantum physics for a second opinion.

On that note, if this seems absurd to you then you are probably not intelligent enough or operating on a level of awareness which is up to par for the vampiric path and you should just pack your bags and move along immediately.

For some this may be new found information that modern science has uncovered, lifting a veil of awareness to something greater than that of the gross physical world which is nothing more than a constant state of material decay. However, certain of the most ancient religions known to man, have known intimately the secrets of the non-physical realm which lie beyond the gate of the gross material world for thousands of years. In fact, as far back as the history of human civilization takes us.

When considering the projection of astral tendrils, an analysis of the above would deem ever fruitful in a further understanding of how the astral body relates to the physical and also how it might be manipulated by force of concentrated will power.

The astral body is slightly larger than the physical body, vibrating at a different frequency, also known as the subtle body. This can, when harnessed, be utilized as a vessel for the higher consciousness to maneuver outside of the body in its non-material form.

When in a state of astral awareness, concentrate on one part of the astral body, typically the solar plexus or the third eye, although it may be the hand or fingers etc., what have you.

From this focal point begin envisioning your astral body extending to the location with which you wish to make contact. This is done by use of will power alone, projecting the consciousness outward through the astral tendril towards the target prey. Continue this as often as needed until results have been successfully achieved, and blood essence has been drained from target.

Vampiric Sadism

We will now expand on vampiric feeding via physical infliction which is a more extreme form of predatory practice.

In the first part of this MS we discussed how the astral body is used to devour blood current from the victim. In this section, we will discuss the practice of vampirism on a much more physical level which does not necessarily use the astral body itself but instead feeds in a more direct manner. When a human experiences extreme physical pain they release a tremendous amount of blood essence, which can be heavily fed upon by the vampire. The amount of blood current released through physical pain or actual blood shed is paramount compared to that of the more accepted and "popular" forms of vampirism.

Remember! The more extreme the physical pain the more the blood current that is released... Use your own discretion on this note and FEED! FEED! FEED!...deeply...

Now, of course, we would *never* advocate crime, but it should be known that the most intense and direct form of feeding via physical infliction is of course the culling of your victim.

When their final breath leaves the body along with their blood essence, where does this go? Straight into the astral field as a free-for-all for whomever may be lurking in wait. If you are to feed through this practice, make sure to draw in the blood current at the apex of subjected treatment, to whatever degree that may extend.

Again, we would *never* suggest anything illegal; this is just for "information purposes." All good little boys and girls who obey the law and pray to jesus go to heaven....

On another note concerning physical vampirism via the auspices of sadism: the practice of blood storage or "occupance" for controlled and long lasting resources. It should be desired and sought after by the vampire to hold a steady resource of blood current, for example a slave.

Himmler practiced this form of large scale vampirism from within the confines of the sinister concentration camps of Nazi Germany, as did Beria from the confines of the hellish gulags of the Soviet Union. In both cases, there was a storage of specimens from which could be forced to be used as slaves as required.

Furthermore, storage of humans equals a storage of Blood Current which can be "spiked" into at any time as necessary for feeding purposes.

Human slavery and sexual deviance via domination is a fine example of vampiric sadism and control...

Marquis De Sade
1740-1814

Oneiric Blood Predator

Moving on, we will now discuss hunting through astral projection and oneiric predation. The vampire hunts instinctively; just like a tiger hunts its prey for survival, so does the living vampire. The vampire, however, is not like an animal in its hunting because where a tiger can only hunt while physically pursuing its prey, the vampire can, in addendum, hunt while he is sleeping and/or in altered conscious/subconscious states.

The predator, while in deep states of meditation, may project his consciousness out of the body, using the astral body as a vehicle. While projected in a deep state of meditation, the predator may remain conscious and keep total control over what and how the projected shadow goes about its hunting. The astral shadow directly responds via pure will power; if the vampire wills the astral body to take wolf-like shape, it will respond immediately.

In the case of oneiric (of/or in relation to dreams) hunting, the experience will be very much the same. Often in dreams, the vampire will find himself hunting and violently attacking humans and drinking their blood. As well, it is not out of the ordinary for the vampire to simply commit heinous acts of murder and abuse in his dreams while not specifically vampirizing them or drinking their blood. Dreams will be flooded on a regular basis with punishment, torture, abuse, murder, blood and other violent scenarios, all of which are perpetrated by their own hands. While in a dream state one may realize consciousness and assume lucid oneiric hunting, which would then be nearly identical to the case of the astral projected self - hunting in response to will.

Psycho-Terror Vampiric Feeding

We will now endeavor to explain the practice of vampirism through emotional and psychological predation. These two methods can be interwoven in use to achieve best results and satiate the Higher Taste. A perfect example of these two methods used in unison is Interrogation, specifically the more "extreme" forms of interrogation such as exercised by extremist political regimes and criminal organizations, where the very real threat of the person's life or that of their family is on the line unless they surrender to the interrogator.

Emotional vampirism can be perpetrated through the creation of certain, usually personal relationships where a strong sense of sympathy is genuinely felt by the victim for the vampire because of certain scenarios which have been orchestrated to make the victim feel sorry for, or want to keep giving and giving to the vampire. This is called emotional vampirism because the vampire is using emotional weight to draw in his victim for whatever manipulation purposes he pleases.

Psychological vampirism is very similar to emotional vampirism, as it is a matter of "setting the mood" to induce psychological conditions such as paranoia, panic, fear, suicidal tendencies, manic depression, madness, terror, etc., etc... you get the point.

Again, we will mention interrogation as an excellent means of psychological feeding. If you convince someone that there are people watching them for example, you will have succeeded in the inducement of paranoia and fear into your victim from which point, the victim may take refuge in you as a "friend to trust" while you continue to elevate his paranoia and delusions, resulting in psychological breakdown. The continuance of inducing psychological ailments and reverse conditions into your victim is a preferred method of feeding as it is drawn out and increasingly incremented in the degree of extremity as time goes on.

Furthermore, psychological vampirism can be perpetrated through acts of subversive manipulation, brainwashing and "assisted" psychological suicide. The latter is referring to the aftermath of a scenario which is in a cold and calculated manner created to usurp the victim's mental stability, along with any sort of "sureness" or self-esteem they may have. This may lead to insanity or self-destruction if committed in perfection.

Black Holes in the Flesh

The living, breathing Undead, who hunt among the human sheep in Godlike form. We make synonymous this type of High Vampire with a black hole because of the natural dark gift to draw many unto them, like a sinistral blood vortex. Certain vampires operating on a Godlike platform often take their place as charismatic leaders within social, political and communal institutions and structures. Often both loved and feared simultaneously to a great degree by their followers, as stated earlier within this manuscript, the Vampire assumes a fearful reign of power over others within their purview. The Vampire Godhead within these institutions and structures, may be found worshipped as being next to God, or even as God himself, within the context of how "God" may be perceived from the perspective of those following or worshipping the hidden Vampire.

Charles Manson was worshipped as a God, was he not? And was he not also both loved and feared by the members of his "family"? Most definitely he was for most certain... Charles Manson used charisma to "win over" those he was grooming to be family members, used drugs, mind control tactics and general vampiric practices to rule his congregation on a Godlike platform.

Father, lover, God and nightmare, Charlie was all of the above to his congregation and was in fact, just as Rev. Jim Jones stated, whatever they wanted him to be. He was whatever his people made him to be. If they saw him as their father, he would be their father. If they saw him as their savior, he would be their savior. If they saw him as their lover, he would be their most intimate lover. And if they feared him, he would be their worst nightmare.

After decades of Charles Manson's federal imprisonment and isolation, still there are many Manson Family members, as well as other fanatics just waiting for Charlie to get out of prison or to "give the word", any word at all, to do his bidding. This bit of history is a very fine example of the walking black hole.

122 yf
Tempel ov the Black Vampire

The Supernal Predator

The Supernal Predator is an acausal non-being of a divine nature that is beyond cosmic limitations and the universal superstructures of Maya. Much like the Sumerian primal chaos dragon Tiamat, and the Indian Death Goddess Kali, The Supernal Predator is the source of origin and of final destination for all things. This divine wamphyric powerhouse of negative black energy can be found under different names from various cultures and is often identified as being the All-Consuming, All- Controlling Darkness beyond the duality of light and dark, creation and destruction.

According to ancient Sumerian mythology, the primal abyss is personified by the chaos dragon MUMMU TIAMAT. Tiamat mixed the 'primordial waters' with her male consort Absu and gave birth to the Elder Gods. Among these was Kingu, the true son of the the Chaos Bloodline. Kingu was the leader of the Legions of Darkness, waging war against the Legions of Light headed by Marduk. In the Enuma Elish, Tiamat and Kingu are slayed by Marduk who in turn used the blood of Kingu to spawn the human race, unbeknownst that the ancient bloodline of Darkness would be carried on within those who have been awakened to their Vampiric Origin. Tiamat is the great womb, origin of all things divine and otherwise. She was first before the Gods of creation and shall remain once all creation has been annihilated. If this is so, creation and/or the material existence will eventually die and flow backwards into the hungry belly of the Dragon – the primal womb of void. In this sense, Tiamat is the All-Consuming Darkness without end, and therefore according to Sumerian mythos, the Supreme Vampire; for all of life and creation in totality shall be consumed.

In the Vedic mythos we generally see three different divine incarnations or "Godheads" which all share the same origin or root word for their names: Kali, Kala and Krsna. All three names translate to "Black" or "Black One". Much like Tiamat, Kali is the great womb of origin from which all emerged and shall descend back into. She is beyond material causal existence and shall ultimately devour the cosmic matrix, vampirizing the core of life itself. In the Devi Mahatmyam, Kali is mentioned when Durga is battling with the demon Raktabija. Every time Durga would attack Raktabija with her sword and spill blood, clones of the demon would rise from the blood drops. This goes on for a while until Durga becomes so enraged by her inability to kill Raktabija that the fearsome Kali emerges from the forehead of Durga as the Goddess's internal Killing Potency. Armed with sword and noose, Kali begins viciously slaughtering Raktabija. Every drop of blood which fell, Kali devoured until she became frenzied in outright blood lust and began killing and drinking the blood of everything she saw.

"Out of the surface of Durga's forehead, fierce with frown, issued suddenly Kali of terrible countenance, armed with a sword and noose. Bearing the strange khatvanga decorated with a garland of skulls, clad in a tiger's skin, very appalling owing to her emaciated flesh, with gaping mouth, fearful with her tongue lolling out, having deep reddish eyes, filling the regions of the sky with her roars, falling upon impetuously and slaughtering the great asuras in that army, she devoured those hordes of the foes of the devas."

Kala, or Mahakala, is one of the many names of Shiva the destroyer and is the masculine form of the name Kali. Kala translates literally to "black" or "time." Time is often interpreted as DEATH and vice versa, for they hold the same meaning. "Time" or death, consumes all things, therefore Kala is a Supreme Vampire, Supernal Predator of all life. Having said that however, Kali will in the end devour Kala, thus devouring even death.

Krsna, whose name means "Dark one" or "Black one", is revered by his worshippers as being the Supreme Personality of Godhead. Krsna is the personification of Darkness before light and space-time, and the emittance of both. Krsna in his first expansion is known as Ananta or Sankarshana, the black energy that is the abyss itself called Tamasi.

Some formidable notes on Lord Ananta as follows:

Ananta is the first and foremost expansion of Lord Krsna.

Ananta awakens lustful longings in women.

Deceives mundane men by keeping the ignorant in ignorance, illusion of ego, "I am the enjoyer of the Universe."

Ananta is worshipped by Shiva, Lord of Destruction. Because of this, Ananta is known as Tamasi (Darkness).

Ananta is the source of, and is at the heart of Shiva.

Ananta wishes to destroy the cosmos. When the time of devastation comes, Ananta transmits the power and knowledge to Shiva on how to destroy the cosmos.

Ananta's name means endless.

Ananta is a massive pre-cosmic serpent with thousands of hooded cobra heads and mouths.

When Ananta uncoils, creation emits. When Ananta coils up, the cosmos are devastated.
Ananta when angered, releases Rudra from his brow to destroy the world.

Anantadeva is equated with primordial darkness and is

the personification of the formless primordial ocean.

Anantadeva's main mission is to dissolve this material creation.

Ananta is King of the Nagas (Snake King).

Thus is the sinister mantra of the Black One

HARE KRSNA HARE KRSNA
KRSNA KRSNA HARE HARE
HARE RAMA HARE RAMA
RAMA RAMA HARE HARE

Krsna is one of the many names of Vishnu and vice versa, and is mentioned in the Bhagavat Gita in chapter 11 as being a most fearful God with terrible devouring flaming jaws.

"*Chapter 11, Verse 25.*
    "O Lord of lords, O refuge of the worlds, please be gracious to me. I cannot keep my balance seeing thus Your blazing deathlike faces and awful teeth. In all directions I am bewildered."

Chapter 11, Verse 26-27.
    "All the sons of Dhrtarastra along with their allied kings, and Bhisma, Drona and Karna, and all our soldiers are rushing into Your mouths, their heads smashed by Your fearful teeth. I see that some are being crushed between Your teeth as well."

Chapter 11, Verse 29.

"I see all people rushing with full speed into Your mouths as moths dash into a blazing fire."

Chapter 11, Verse 30.

"O Visnu, I see You devouring all people in Your flaming mouths and covering the universe with Your immeasurable rays. Scorching the worlds, You are manifest."

Tyrant Nirrta
126 yf

Ocean of Blood

Thick dew began to form on the ground around him as the early morning neared 3AM. He had been standing there for hours in a sort of coma-like trance. To an outsider it might appear as if he had died while standing there. Perhaps he did... Luckily for him this was a deserted and isolated place, free of interrupting life forms for miles. He had picked this place wisely, or rather it was picked for him from the very force he sought and who guided him there.

He had been calling out to her from inside, reaching deeper than his very soul. He did not use words, for words could neither describe nor could sounds comprehend her glorious sinistral power. Time ceased to exist as he drifted through astral vortexes searching for her. Perhaps he had always been in this place and his so-called life was just a minor "speed bump" in his pursuit. At this point who was to know, who was to tell?

He heard a whisper echoing through the astral vortexes which he now explored, though the sound was not like a sound you would hear with your ears, it was more like a brainwave or an external impulse. The whisper was elongated and distorted as if breaking through a natural border of causal experience and seemed to carry on. It was his   name.

Before he could respond, he felt pulled back to what

seemed to be where he had been standing for the last several hours. He opened his eyes to what should have been a forested landscape but instead saw only blackness. When his eyes regained proper vision he began to see a glow off in the distance. A glow which neither consisted of color, nor was it white. Instead, an atmosphere of relentless cold emanated from the glow. Looking closer, or perhaps it was moving towards him, he could see that it was not one glow but in fact were two piercing cold, black crystallized eyes which seemed to stare right through him.

He felt a cold hand touch his naked shoulder and immediately begin to drain him of his human life. Turning around to face his great and terrible Mother, his entire body became soaked in cold sweat. Seeing only her black eyes, countless nightmarish visions of demonic beings and abyssal landscapes were shown to him. One of which being the end of his own life. The cold sweat swept over him like a hurricane rain and he felt as though he was submerged into liquid. Closing his eyes as to look away from the nightmarish visions for a moment and reopening them, he saw only a vast sea of blood without horizon or end. He found himself drowning in the black blood abyss in an attempt to save his life, but it was too late.

In life he loathed existence, and when he opened himself to Satan, he sought Lilith to guide him through his transformation of inner alchemy. He wanted to find his place beside the Lord in the Kingdom of Hell. Tonight Lilith answered his prayers. He would step beyond existence   and   enter   the   abyss   willing   or   not.

Struggling and suffocating, the endless black and crimson ocean poured down his throat and into his lungs. His body became heavier and his chest began to burn, he now drifted down into the sea of no end, giving in to his fate, abandoning all hope and leaving life behind.

The burning in his chest intensified and seemed to spread throughout his body as he fell deeper, he could see Lilith looking at him, the eyes reflecting darkness down into the ocean from the non-descript black sky like duel eclipses. His body ignited into black flames as he now began to ascend back to the surface. Rising from the sea, the flames slithered around his body like snakes devouring and casting aside his flesh. No longer did he exist, rising as pure fire from the sea of blood and forming into burning wings. The invisible rising fire transcended the causal going beyond the abyss leaving the former in ashes...

Tyrant Nirrta
119 yf
Tempel ov the Black Vampire

The Program; Alchemical Change Process

Traditional Black Vampirism has been for the most part an oral tradition passed down since the beginning of time. As an example, the first written records date back to the early Aryan Vedic and Sumerian period, several thousand years ago. Vampirism played a major role in both above stated civilizations and still does to this day. Interestingly, this is literally thousands of years before the name Satan even existed, to put things into perspective.

In all ancient religions you will easily find varying adaptations of these Dark Gods who descended to earth and mixed with the human race in those designated early regions, creating offspring carrying the dark bloodline. Because of the Godlike origin, this bloodline has been identified as not only an ancestral blood lineage passed down through thousands of years, but also a spiritual bloodline which is capable of being accessed much like how one would tap into a tree to milk the internal nectar. On this note, that being the Alchemical Change Process, it is a matter of emptying the sour milk inside the human host and tapping into the internal nectar of that which we came from ,which is all around us at all times. The black swirling energy vortex that begot even our demonic ancestors from the stars, which the ancient Aryan nations spoke of.

Call it what you will: Tiamat, Ginnungagap, Nythra, Krsna, or the Abyss. The Black, like a negative pulse, is the blood that forged our ancestors. The Dark Immortals.

The program for the creation of the new being is a metamorphic transformation of the initiate's psyche, spirit and bloodline. The blood of the undead is of the most ancient origin, that being the supersoul of primeval darkness. The Vampiric Supersoul is none other than the vacuous abyss of precreation, personified as the Black One.

While some are born to the ancient vampiric bloodline, others may be inducted via blood baptism and harsh alchemical change process. In order for the Vampire to rise from the mundane human shell, the human must first experience physical and psychological trauma, pain, suffering and imminent death to unblock the path of undead rebirth. This is not something to take for granted, nor should it be underestimated. Most will not make it through this extreme transition, merely becoming food for the ever hungry, churning blood abyss. Let it be made clear, with no uncertainty that the illusive sense of self will be shattered, casting the ego into the destructive fires of transformation. Only then will the incessant crimson "reign of mercy" wash over you like pounding waves from the poison ocean of God.

The Program, or Alchemical Change Process, is a system with which the initiate forges his rites of passage into the black dynasty of the blood pool via violent internalized force and a myriad of psycho-political programming methods. ACP rapidly releases the initiate of the previous deeply rooted systems of human moral obligations and thought processes, enabling the "cup" or human host to spill out its contents to make way for the dark energies of the bloody abyss to assume control for the greater glory of the Dark Immortals. One must with fanatical will, and internal negative magnetic drive, serve the dark to become one with them.

The Vampire is not concerned with sympathy or compassion for others, nor does He lower himself to raise up another. Bereft of compassion to life, being of a demonic breed of the Nightside, the Vampire is no stranger to the grim solace found in the art of illusion, persuasion, and manipulation of the human herd. They are the pawns in the sinister game of cat and mouse for which the Vampire is the Lion of the dark underworld.

The Vampire holds no allegiance to, nor abides by the laws of any human law-biding organization and/or government. Traditional Vampirism rejects all systems of law which would stand against the law of the vampire. The Law of the Vampire is Lawlessness.

Are you on The Program?

Tyrant Nirrta
126 yf

THE BLACK ART OF CRIME

"Corruption, thou art thy father"

Our Father, who art in Hell,
Unhallowed be thy Name.
Thy kingdom come.
Thy will be done,
On earth as it is in Hell.
Give us this night our nightly blood.
And empower us through our trespasses,
As we devour those who trespass against us.
Lead us down into the altars of Hell,
And deliver us to evil.

The Ethos of Criminality

Black Vampirism is quintessentially criminal in nature in terms of spirituality, religion, and the real-world arena.

Vampirism has, since time immemorial, been the most hideous and illicit mode of existence. A path most certainly less travelled by very select few. Saved for those without a sense of moral, or lawful obligation towards a weak-willed system of the white lodge and its cattle.

It was not until in recent years with the emergence of these soft, limp-wristed pseudo-intellectuals and homosexuals calling themselves "vampires", and claiming sole authorship to the history of Vampirism for all time. Those who adhere strictly to the laws of the cattle state, support and hold hands with law enforcement, do their very best to make "vampirism" safe and acceptable publicly, and frown upon any and all harm, discomfort or mistreatment of the human race...

Vampirism is not a goth subculture, nor is it anything to do with an Anton Lavey church or some other white lodge nonsense.

We evoke the use of the term Black Vampirism not only to clearly separate us in opposition of extreme prejudice to these bourgeois sheep in wolves' clothing, but also to set the tone. The tone of Traditional Black Vampirism. That which is absolutely free of moral, or lawful obligation. The

Black Vampire is an enemy of the state seeking the total downfall and involution of all. Solvet saeclum in favilla...

The blood of the world is what feeds us. One dominates and destroys its prey, laughing maniacally as it chokes. Uttering bitter mockeries at its pathetic existence and ultimate demise.

The Black Vampire is Ultra-Negative, thus, Black.

Now that the distinction has been made we will move along...

Spirituality:

The spiritual essence of criminality is limitless and without borders, which would otherwise chain the dark spirit to the gross material plane. Those bound by the ethereal constructs of peace seeking, loving thy neighbour and the general mode of goodness exist with a chain of fear around their neck. This metaphorical chain being much like a noose with which the end of the rope is in the hand of an agent of the mode of darkness whilst the knot tightens. Like a dog on a leash the virtuous are as prey to those who are not hindered by the spiritual chains of morality, geniality and goodness.

The spirit of darkness does not hide behind reflections of the light and its agents of goodness, nay. The Spirit of Darkness casts a shadow with utmost authority and everlasting affliction which snuffs out every glint of light under its fathomless leathern wings.

The spirit of the Black Vampire is none other than the reflection of the supreme Spirit of Darkness itself and the vacuum beyond the matrix of space and time from which its origins took root tooth and nail. The singularity, known to some as The Dark One, The Abyss, Tamasi, Ginnungagap and Hell.

Religion:

He whose ears fall deaf on the word of "God" is considered a criminal in the eyes of the white lodge ministries and their leaders. A blasphemer, a transgressor and a demon. Let's not be confused either - that inherently is the intention. It is our pledge to Darkness that twists and churns our path from the straight and narrow to the crooked, corrupt and backwards mysteries that lurk in the shadows of the razor's edge.

The Lord of Darkness is the ultimate trespasser in all realms of every religious doctrine that has ever existed or shall ever exist. The Devil is the great opposer of the sons of light and transgressor of the laws of their God; the highest priest in the divine ministry of the fallen, who wages violent war against the angelic state and their senate. Of all criminals, our Dark Lord is the greatest and most corrupt of all, having autocratic ordinance and greatest supremacy entirely.

*** *** ***

"And Manasseh turned aside his heart to serve Belial; for the angel of lawlessness, who is the ruler of this world, is Belial, whose name is Matanbuchus.

—*(Ascension of Isaiah 2:4)"*

In the above quote we can see a very direct correlation between the Lord of Darkness and lawlessness according to judeo-xian religion. For is the Dark Lord not the adversary? Most certainly He is, and of the highest degree.

Satan, our Great Dragon Prince of Darkness is a name given to Him within the judeo religious system which translates from Hebrew to "Enemy." It is distinctly clear why such became the name for which He is addressed in that tradition. Satan is also called Belial, meaning "without god" or "without law." Thus Satan, who is called Belial, is the God of lawlessness, corruption and death.

"Let us rejoice in the corruption of the earth
For therein lies the fruits of our seed
The negative pulse of worthless night
Corrupting the seed and sons of light
He who stands before all thrones yet bows to none
He who comes as the enemy to burn the sons of Israel
He whose dominion entombs the cold earth
He who from the North sets fire to the world
And for corruption himself hath been given the name Belial
For He is the Lord of Lawless Destruction
And the origin of the seed of corruption...

Ave Dominus Belial in Excelsis!"
- Corruption Prayer-
Tempel ov the Black Vampire

The rays of light cast from the heavens calculate and define everything they touch. In this manner they simultaneously set restrictions on how the definitions of those calculations are perceived from the matter they touch which intrinsically create laws of space-time and physics instantly and inseparably attached to that matter.

In that mirror image, the rays of darkness which ascend from the endless abyss below counter, corrupt, destroy and turn black the restricting, law-abiding rays of light, setting free lawless darkness to murder the light.

An adversary to the foundations of not only life itself, but the very fabric of space-time which make up the vast, calculable and definitive universe(s). Under this non-life affirming scope, the Dark Lord could be understood as the greatest terrorist (Terror Incarnate) on a cosmic scale, setting fire to all the worlds in every direction while simultaneously devouring them whole.

*** *** ***

"Chapter 11, Verse 30, Bhagavad Gita

O Viṣṇu, I see You devouring all people in Your flaming mouths and covering the universe with Your immeasurable rays. Scorching the worlds, you are manifest."

"Chapter 11, Verse 32, Bhagavad Gita

The Blessed Lord said: Time I am, destroyer of the worlds, and I have come to engage all people."

In the quoted verses above we see the Vedic Aryan god Visnu, more often identified as Krsna, being observed incarnating as cosmic annihilation personified and with savage, endless hunger. Krsna is worshipped by vast numbers all throughout the world. It is believed, with various discoveries of ancient statues and artifacts found globally to back this theory up, that at one time the entire world was under collective Vedic religious thought.

While the majority of people who employ devotional service to Krsna do so recognizing only His benign aspects and make claims that Krsna is just a peaceful and gracious God of light.

In reality, these claims are quite absurd at best. Krsna for example literally translates to Black One, being the personification of the primordial darkness of nothingness. In this incarnation He is known as Tamasi (Darkness). It is Tamasi who instructs the terrible forms of Rudra (Bhairava / Nirrta) in how to incinerate and annihilate the entire universe.

There are countless examples of divine criminality in the Vedas, specifically of the Vaishnava sort concerning several expansions of Krsna, Kali and Rudra. Many have taken one or all of these Gods as their Patron God(s) of Crime and demonic pastimes in order to serve the omnipotent malign darkness. Bhairava for example, whose name translates to "Terror" is the epitome of, and is the personification of religious crime in the Vedas. In the Origin Myth of the Brahmanicide, Bhairava decapitates the head of Brahma, the God of creation. This is the highest crime possible in the Vedic religion. Bhairava is also called Nirrta which literally translates to "No Law."

Some might say that Nirrta is the Vedic equivalent to Belial of the judeo-christian system. Both have a name with the very exact same meaning and both also personify the qualities and actualization of malignant darkness, corruption and death. Not to say that they are the same thing, but in fact within their own separate religious designations they are identical in their personified execution of sinister pastimes .

*

The word Thug which is so widely used today to describe criminals and gangsters, either as derogatory or self-appointed (i.e. "Thug Life"), actually has a very legitimate origin. Dating back to early 1300s CE, the Cult of Thuggees terrorized India for nearly 500 years. They engaged in devotional service to the Annihilation Goddess of Darkness, Kali Ma, via acts of terror, sinister pastimes including robbery, kidnapping and murder all in the name of the Aryan Blood Goddess.

The word Thug or Thuggee, translates from Hindi as Deceiver. The cult would deceive travellers by tricking them into their company, fraudulently befriending them, robbing their belongings, then finally kidnapping and/or murdering them, usually the latter.

In their active near 500 year terror, it is believed they murdered upwards of two-million people. The Thugs were the first Mafia to exist in the world, and due to the extremity of their crimes, the most homicidal terrorist organization with the highest death toll in history to date.

*

There is a tantric cult also from India, the Aghoris, who still exist to this day. They practice their own form of transgressive spirituality. The history of the Aghoris is unclear as there were never any kind of records kept within the cult. An oral tradition of old passing their secrets from guru to devotee in succession for generations upon generations.

Found in few areas around the world, their most well-known place of dwelling is the Bombay cremation grounds near the Ganges River. It is said that the pyres of Bombay have been burning nonstop for a thousand years.

The Aghoris (A-ghora = without-terror, fearless) are Saivites/Shaivaites. They worship the Tantric God of Destruction SHIVA and consort, the Blood Goddess KALI MA. Their mode is tamasic and their speciality is in extremism. They live in the cremation grounds detached and cut off from the world with their bodies covered head to toe in the ashes of the dead. The Aghoris drink the blood and eat the flesh of the living and dead – including humans. Murder is ordinary and heavy intoxication (excessive amounts of alcohol and ganga) is constant. They eat and drink from a human skull called a Kapala.

They believe that by gorging on filth and engaging in transgressive, amoral, violent and illegal acts, they become free from the attachments to separation from the ParaBrahman, detaching themselves from the enchaining karma, thus becoming closer to God.

As an example of freeing themselves from the attachments to separation, they will drink urine, eat feces or rotten human flesh with the same lack of concern as if they were to eat a piece of chocolate cake. To them, there is no difference between the two. Likewise, no difference between the living and the dead, for Lord Shiva has already claimed them all in their final destination.

*** *** ***

In South America, the recent rise of the Narco Cult of Death is another very good example of criminality in religion. The patron saint of Holy Death or San la Muerte, who is revealed as the Grim Reaper. A pale skeletal figure cloaked in a robe and holding a scythe. There are three basic colours that San la Muerte appears in: White, red and black. White for works of goodness, red for works of passion and black for the works of sorcery and protection. It is the black form that has quickly forged this narco death cult. The cults' demographic being mostly of the unlawful sort. Those living in poverty, social outcasts and those living in the dark underbelly of society. Drug Cartels for example will pay homage to their dark skeletal protector to keep them safe from their enemies, to ensure safe delivery of drugs to drop spots, to bring tidings of money and to bring harm to those who would try to harm them with increased violence.

Death does not pick and choose who it takes; Death takes all and turns no one away. This is, in part, largely the reason for its rapid growth. SLM Cult of Death does not judge its followers or discern any difference in them whatsoever for their life choices, as opposed to Catholicism.

"The Santa Muerte cult is anti-establishment and appears to glorify criminal behavior. Although not all members of the cult are criminals, all live an existence that is dominated by crime. The cult seems to be linked closely to prisons, prisoners, and family members of prisoners. It is also associated with at least two organized criminal groups – the Gulf Cartel and the Mara Salvatrucha. Although it does not appear that most practitioners would commit crimes on behalf of the cult, some criminals might use it as an impetus to commit a crime or to increase the scale and violence of their crimes. Furthermore, because of the inherent danger in crime, the invocation of death itself as patron has a manifest appeal."

-Kevin Freese,
Foreign Military Studies Office, Fort Leavenworth, KS.

Black Arts of Crime

The vampiric disciples of the Hellfire Ministries, being criminally inclined by bloodline and birthright on every level, in terms of universal "morals" and "laws" specifically among others, typically find natural calling to anti-social or criminal lifestyles. As such, just as any genuine psychopath (Mastermind) will seek the heights of their exquisite and awful abilities in one degree or another.

As has been stated before and should already be known as truth without need for mentioning, the vampire holds no law of Man above its own nor does it kowtow to institutional, state, political or White Lodge religious obedience formats. Often finding symbiosis with outcasts, outlaws or other underground affiliations, associations and clandestine groups, or sometimes solely in isolation.

Elements of destructive energies and corruption can take form on an entire spectrum from white to black. Often originating from righteousness or good intentions "The road to Hell is paved with good intentions" - or more appropriately with sinister origin and intent. An example from history is the Inquisition. People who had "good" intentions of religious righteousness with intent to rid itself of evil in turn becoming that which they were trying to conquer. Leaving a horrifically brutal and torturous, homicidal imprint on the history of human civilization.

Everywhere in the world in history and modern times there are and have been wars waged over religious righteousness, resulting in rivers of blood spilled by the wrathful with "good intentions."

The blood of the living makes good fertilizer for the seeds of the new

And with every drop, the Dark Lord is given sacrifice and served...

The soldiers and enforcers of the benign faiths of the world may not escape the vanity of their mission and the evil resolve which equates from them. The spirit of Darkness reigns over the world and WILL exact its will in anyway which presents itself. Especially those which seek to destroy it. Corruption is at the heart of man, for the entire ideal of peace is fraudulent; creation itself was forged in violence. Just as every other life molecule in the existent cosmic structure, the human race shall also succumb to incremented decay, devastation and ultimate violent annihilation till the Darkness opens its wings of emptiness and returns to its ancient womb.

*** *** ***

There exists a clandestine network not dissimilar to a deadly spider web which operates on an international scale, an organized criminal network which could be likened to a sort of satanic mafia. Its "Godfather" being the personification of darkness and evil himself, our Lord and Father the Devil.

The disciples of this clandestine legion take office in high politics, law firms, religious institutions, government intelligence agencies, military, police force, organized crime syndicates, terrorist and revolutionary organizations of the far left and far right. They can also be found working in schools teaching your children and watching them in daycare centers, rolling with street gangs, guarding your homes or cooking your meals...

...Always waiting, always watching, never sleeping...

In this section however, we are specifically exploring the criminal element and certain common practices which from a vampiric perspective, will ascertain its high degree of real-world utility within the black arts of vampirism.

Money has been notoriously noted as the root of all evil for hundreds of years, and not without reason. Money is in reality an illusory currency without substance, yet it carries with it a substantial weight of consequence. For some it is a doorway to possibilities unreachable by many, for most it is an enslaving tyrannical servitude, for all it is the main ingredient in the five course meal of greed and corruption. In modern times, money has even replaced god in some parts of the world.

It is this paper gasoline that has fueled the world of organized crime, allowing groups to seize and control neighbourhoods and larger territories such as entire countries. Let there be no confusion, money means nothing from a vampiric perspective. It is just as worthless as its judeo originators; it does however have its utilities when harbored correctly. As an example - more blood has been spilled in the world over monetary wealth than any political cause or religious God. It has been, is, and continues to be the cause for the sanctioning of murder, strife and war world wide. Humans and life itself is bought and sold like cattle at farming auctions.

Drugs are a poisonous rose with a thorn ridden collar, recreational death at an upside down fair ground, a slave master with a razor tooth grin. The depths of addiction go all the way down the spiral staircase to Hell. Selling hard drugs is an excellent business choice for the vampiric adherent, as it enables you to profit from the user in exchange for life-altering highly destructive chemicals and then continue to feed from their ruination till they look like the walking dead. Literally drain the life from them. There is really no limit to how far you want to take this; how many people do you know that like to party?

Ideally you should aim to retain as many users as possible, coming to you for their taste of sweet death and slavery. Going further, retain underlings to put the footwork in for you after you have put in significant time learning the trade inside and out. This will quickly launch you into truly living life on the edge. As per insight and sinister capabilities, the sky is the limit. This line of work as a vampiric objective is certainly not for the faint of heart as the ugliness, filth, disparity, and true identity of those you think you know will be revealed to you with likely very adverse results. Any trust or sense of loyalty of others will without a doubt be crushed with heavy steel-toed boots. Be prepared to sever or lose many personal relationships or brotherhood you might have because it will be the ones closest to you that will betray you... a note of forewarning... this is a true predatory trade.

Intimidation, fear and terror as methods to enforce dominance, vulnerability and obedience under fear of consequences have been tried, tested and true since the beginning of mankind. A police officer exerts dominance over the public to enforce government laws or "order" under fear of monetary fines, martial law, imprisonment, brutality or death. Revolutionary and terrorist groups will use terror against their targets to instill fear, terror and instability. Nations exert political or military power over other nations under fear of take-over, nuclear attack, enslavement or death. Corporations exert intimidation over competitors and smaller companies. Gangs or other organized crime syndicates exert dominance over other gangs and similar groups under fear of brutality and death. The wolf hunts the deer and the snake strangles the rabbit and so on and so forth.

Gangsters will use intimidation for example when doing collections for drug debts and extortion, when the person who owes will be "taxed." The tax can be a very high added interest rate, i.e. 50 to 1000% is not unusual. The tax might be a onetime added amount often known as "asshole tax" or it could simply mean getting the living shit beaten   out   of   you   or   worse...

Blackmail is an excellent and essential asset to keep in mind, whether you ever use it or not, just to keep things...square. If you are actively engaged in unlawful activities and meet someone along the way who knows it, especially if that individual appears to have some kind of interest in "teaming up" with you, the first thing you want to do before anything is to incriminate them in some kind of unlawful deed, intoxicant or other crime that you can use to incriminate them with if such a day came to needing to have that kind of "insurance." To reiterate, if one car crashes, so does the other automatically; a form of insurance or security net to keep on the back burner when operating in the underbelly of society.

Blackmail can also be used as a tool of leverage to force cooperation or obedience of someone against their will under fear of being exposed, usually something about them or an act committed that could jeopardize their reputation among family, friends, business associates or general public, i.e. maybe they are involved in identity theft, pedophilia, caught committing adultery with pictures being withheld of the act as leverage. Perhaps they were caught in the act of some kind of unlawful offence and coerced into ratting out their associates by the pigs that be, or even have members of their family being held against their will in an unknown location until some kind of activity is completed to further monetary gain for the   captors   in   question.

FINIS

Printed in Great Britain
by Amazon

55891198R00036